...of the United States in or...

...for the common defence, promote the general Wel...

...stablish this Constitution for the United States of...

The sacred rights of mankind are not to be rummaged for among old
parchments or musty records. They are written, as with a sun beam,
in the whole volume of human nature by the hand of the divinity itself;
and can never be erased or obscured by mortal power.

ALEXANDER HAMILTON
The Farmer Refuted

Hall of the House of Burgesses, Colonial Williamsburg, Virginia

What influence in fact have ecclesiastical establishments had on Civil Society? In some instances they have been seen to erect a spiritual tyranny on the ruins of Civil authority; in many instances they have been seen upholding the thrones of political tyranny; in no instance have they been seen the guardians of the liberties of the people.

JAMES MADISON
Memorial and Remonstrance [8]

5709 N. 20th Street, Ridgefield, WA 98642 • (360) 857-7040 • www.NRLA.com • ISBN 978-1-5323-5129-7

Photos ©2017 Shutterstock Images, iStockphoto by Getty Images, Gregory W. Hamilton and from the Public Domain.
Book Design: PalimorDesignStudios.com • Printed in China

TABLE OF CONTENTS

Rediscovering America's Soul 5

The Fight for Religious Freedom 9

Declaration of Principles 16

The Declaration of Independence 21

The Constitution of the United States 28

Amendments to the Constitution of the United States 42

The Universal Declaration of Human Rights 50

Championing Religious Freedom & Human Rights
For All People & Institutions of Good Will 52

Our Philosophy 54

Serving You 57

Legislative Advocacy 58

Liberty Magazine: A Resource for Matters
of Religious Freedom and Human Rights 61

Ways You Can Help Protect Religious Liberty 62

It can never be too often repeated that the time for fixing every essential right on a legal basis is while our rulers are honest, and ourselves united.

THOMAS JEFFERSON

4

REDISCOVERING AMERICA'S SOUL

Liberty of Conscience and
the Separation of Church and State

When Roger Williams the colonial founder of Rhode Island wrote his treatise known as "The Bloody Tenent" in 1636, he had no idea how his radical challenge to the Puritan Divines – of separating the institutions of church and state – would end up influencing America's Constitutional Founders, and in time revolutionizing Europe and the world.

153 years later, in the sweltering summer of 1789, James Madison penned sixteen words in spare prose that would become America's First Freedom – the religion clauses of the First Amendment to the United States Constitution: "Congress shall make no law respecting an establishment of religion, or prohibiting the free exercise thereof…" As historian Randall Balmer observed in the PBS film, *The Fight for Religious Liberty*: "Herein the founding fathers of a young government pledged separation of church and state, thus guaranteeing religious freedom for its citizens and establishing a free marketplace for religion in the United States. Utterly unprecedented in Western history, this construction of a government without the interlocking authority of religion set a new course for faith and politics and has produced a vibrant religious culture unmatched anywhere in the world."

Soul Liberty: Celebrating America's First Freedom, is a coffee table book that provides a colorful pictorial relief of the progression of religious liberty from Pilgrims and Puritans to the creation of the Bill of Rights and how it shaped a new nation. The Declaration of Independence, the United States Constitution, the Amendments to the Constitution, and the Universal Declaration of Human Rights are provided in a rich and colorful panorama with photos and quotes of the Founders. The primary goal of this book is to rediscover and present America's rich heritage in an exciting new way for the reader and the student – so even a child's curiosity is raised and gradually influenced over time to see the value of these documents, the value of our Constitutional Republic, and the sacred principles of religious freedom and liberty of conscience.

Constitutional religious freedom, the separation of church and state, and liberty of conscience are under threat by all three branches of government. There are many voices today that seek to redefine America's constitutional history, particularly in regard to these vital topics. "Our Philosophy" statement on page 54 briefly explains the dangers that exist when extreme voices present themselves as "truth."

Since 1906, the Northwest Religious Liberty Association has successfully championed religious freedom and human rights for all people and institutions of good will in the states of Alaska, Idaho, Montana, Oregon and Washington. This book is a statement of our principles and philosophy regarding the proper roles of church and state in the effort to preserve and champion true religious freedom. We also provide proven ideas and tools on how you can get involved in championing and defending religious freedom in a thoughtful way. Note especially the panoramic photo of the signing ceremony of the Oregon Workplace Religious Freedom Act with Oregon Governor Ted Kulongoski that occurred on April 1, 2010. Sponsored by the Honorable Dave Hunt, Speaker of the Oregon House of Representatives, the Northwest Religious Liberty Association introduced and shepherded the bill over several years.

Soul Liberty is a book that seeks to educate and inspire. The Northwest Religious Liberty Association and its board of directors headquartered at the Northwest Headquarters of the Seventh-day Adventist Church in Ridgefield, Washington, encourages you, the American Citizen, to make America's "First Freedom" – the free exercise of religion and the constitutional separation of church and state – a renewed priority and personal commitment.

GREGORY W. HAMILTON, PRESIDENT

Northwest Religious Liberty Association

There goes many a ship to sea, with many souls in one ship, whose weal and woe is a true picture of society. Sometimes Papists, Protestants, Jews, and Turks may be embarked in one ship; upon which I affirm that all the liberty of conscience that ever I pleaded for turns upon this: that none be forced to come to the ships prayers or worship, nor be restrained from their own particular prayers or worship, if they practice any.

ROGER WILLIAMS

THE FIGHT FOR RELIGIOUS FREEDOM
America's Journey in Historical Context

America's nascent journey toward religious freedom sprang from both religion and politics. It began with the English Pilgrim Separatists who settled Plymouth Colony upon their arrival on the *Mayflower* in 1620. They were Puritans who broke away from the monarchical Church of England because they felt it had not completed the work of the Protestant Reformation. This, they believed, was because of the church-state unity that corrupted both the state and the church's "separate but holy" duties. The Congregationalist Puritans were given a royal charter to settle what would become the Massachusetts Bay Colony, centered first in Plymouth, and later in Boston. These Puritans accepted some of the customs and rights of the Church of England and defined church-state collaborations for their own holy and utopian societal purposes.

But the seeds of their own unraveling came through their lack of tolerance for dissension. This led to the martyrdom of evangelical pioneer Mary Dyer; the banishment of Anne Hutchinson, the offshoot charismatic home church leader; the subsequent trial and exile of Roger Williams; and the Salem witch trials, in which 20 women and girls were sentenced to death. As Founder of the Colony of Rhode Island, Williams was the inspiration for future Baptist pastors such as Isaac Backus and John LeLand, who would inform and nurture his heretical doctrine of church-state separation in the minds and hearts of America's Revolutionary Founders, particularly Thomas Jefferson and James Madison.

AWAKENING & SEEDS OF REVOLUTION

America's First Great Awakening emerged with the preaching of Jonathan Edwards, the Puritan Divine from Massachusetts, and the itinerant Dutch "field preachers" of the Middle Colonies, who paved the way for the most famous itinerant of all, George Whitefield. He preached the emancipating message that eternal salvation through a "new birth" experience in Christ was available to all – rich and poor alike. What remained constant in both the Puritan and Awakening periods was the cherished idea that America was the new Israel in a new Promised Land – "A city upon a hill," an exceptional phrase coined in the sermon "A Model of Christian Charity" preached on the ship Arabella by Puritan John Winthrop ten years after the Pilgrims landed at Plymouth Rock in 1620. But what changed during the Awakening Period was the inclusion of a revolutionary thought: that salvation was not dependent on a king, a specific denominational polity, or government, but through Christ alone. This message spread throughout all the 13 Colonies and produced a sense of national cohesiveness, and in time religious pluralism. This was largely a charismatic Protestant phenomenon, germinating the spirit of democracy and eventually a new nation that would experiment in a Republican form of government.

Thomas Jefferson's central premise when penning the words of the Declaration of Independence, was that individual rights, equal rights, were inalienable and came from God and not kings: "We hold these truths to be self-evident, that all men are created equal, that they are endowed by their Creator with certain unalienable Rights, that among these are Life, Liberty and the pursuit of Happiness." The very language of Thomas Jefferson's authorship of the Declaration of Independence served in philosophy, message and tone, as an assault on King George III and the so-called divine right of kings. And first among Jefferson's "unalienable rights" was freedom of conscience, because closely connected to the King was a corresponding Monarchical Church, the Church of England, which was loosely but ultimately governed by the King.

Religious Freedom Revolution

Jefferson's Declaration, therefore, served as the People's Declaration against the divine right of both the King and the Church to govern their souls, and by necessary and willful extension their newly declared "United States of America". It was no mere coincidence that one month prior to declaring independence from Britain, Virginia's Declaration of Rights was adopted by Virginia's General Assembly. Contained within this Declaration was a special section that emphasized religious freedom. James Madison declared that "all men are entitled to the free exercise of religion, according to the dictates of conscience." In 1777, it was Thomas Jefferson who drafted what would become Virginia's Statute of Religious Freedom. "Almighty God hath created the mind free; all attempts to influence it by temporal punishments of burdens, or by civil incapacitations, tend only to beget habits of hypocrisy and meanness, and are a departure from the plan of the holy author of our religion, who being Lord both of body and mind, yet chose not to propagate it by coercions on either, as was in His almighty power to do."

And James Madison, in his famous 15-point Memorial & Remonstrance, declared the following in Remonstrance #8: "What influence in fact have ecclesiastical establishments had on Civil Society? In some instances they have been seen to erect a spiritual tyranny on the ruins of Civil authority; in many instances they have been seen upholding the thrones of political tyranny; in no instance have they been seen the guardians of the liberties of the people." Madison's Memorial was a document that lobbied strongly in favor of Jefferson's Statute for Religious Freedom, and against Patrick Henry's "Bill Establishing a Provision for Teachers of the Christian Religion" – a government funding bill that favored the Anglican, or American based Church of England, the majority religion.

Madison reflected on this experience some years later in 1832 in which a similar movement led by the Rev. Jasper Adams was afoot. Adams pressed Madison with the argument that since most Americans were Christian that Christianity in general should be constitutionally recognized and funded by the government in a non-discriminatory way. Mr. Madison responded by writing: "Who does not see that the same authority which can establish Christianity, in exclusion of all other religions, may establish with the same ease any particular sect of Christians in exclusion of all other sects?" And besides, he wrote, "Experience will be an admitted Umpire. In the Papal System, Government and Religion are in a manner consolidated, and that is found to be the worst of Govts." The master historian that he was, Madison was adamant about making sure that all faith groups were protected equally under the law. Religious pluralism would be the engine ensuring democratic ideals. It was the only way.

The Virginia Statute for Religious Freedom is a statement about both freedom of conscience and the principle of separation of church and state. Written by Thomas Jefferson and passed by the Virginia General Assembly on January 16, 1786, it served as the forerunner of the First Amendment protections for religious freedom adopted by the First Congress in 1789, namely that "Congress shall make no law respecting an establishment of religion, or prohibiting the free exercise thereof..." Virginia became the first state to disestablish their state-favored, tax-supported church, and after the ratification of the Constitution and Bill of Rights in 1789 and 1791, respectively, the other states would quickly follow, with Massachusetts being the last of the original 13 states to do so in 1833.

PROTECTING THE PEOPLE FROM THEMSELVES

The conceptual origins of the Constitution of the United States of America began with General Washington around the campfires at Valley Forge during the bitter Revolutionary winter of 1777-1778. Here Alexander Hamilton and John Marshall crafted their dream for a federal government with three separate and co-equal independent branches – the Executive, Legislative and Judicial branches – and a federalist system with checks and balances that included states being semi-autonomous but ultimately answerable to the federal government. Simultaneously, James Madison, dubbed the "Father of the Constitution," was crafting the same formula for America's Post-Revolutionary War experiment in constitutional government. Hamilton's and Madison's federalist dreams were fulfilled at the Constitutional Convention of 1787, held in Independence Hall in Philadelphia. There, the Liberty Bell still reminds Americans that this nation was conceived for Liberty.

But there was a problem. Thomas Jefferson, who was always fearful of unchecked and overbearing powers, argued from Paris that the states should not ratify the newly crafted and signed Constitution until sufficient guarantees were made that a Bill of the people's Rights would be enumerated. Alexander Hamilton resisted such appeals, and so did Madison who argued that since Congress possessed no power to interfere with basic rights, the Constitution alone was enough. But Madison, who was a close friend of Jefferson's, began to see Jefferson's point in their fevered correspondence.

The Constitution's Preamble begins with the words "WE THE PEOPLE of the United States", clearly suggesting that the majority rules. But Jefferson and Madison were fearful of an out-of-control people – the fickle will of "We the People". It was James Madison who eloquently argued that a final check and balance needed to be crafted and ratified – a Bill of Rights that protected the rights of the people against abusive majorities. During the First Congress of 1789 in New York's Federal Hall, across from today's modern-day Wall Street in Manhattan, James Madison rose up during the debate over whether the United States should adopt a Bill of Rights. He said,

"I confess that in a government modified like this of the United States the greater danger lies rather in the abuse of the community than in the legislative body. The prescriptions in favor of liberty ought, therefore, to be leveled against that quarter where the greatest danger lies, namely that which possesses THE HIGHEST PREROGATIVE OF POWER: But this is not found in either the executive or legislative departments of government, but in the body of the people, operating by the majority against the minority."

JAMES MADISON

Proposal of the Bill of Rights to the House of Representatives, First U.S. Congressional Session, June 8, 1789.

The Price of Liberty

As a result, the First Congress agreed to move forward with the sacred task of protecting the rights of "We the People" in an effort to safeguard the people from themselves and in order to ensure the ultimate success of their new constitutional system. The Bill of Rights was happily ratified by the States in 1791.

America's fledgling experience in Republican and Democratic forms of government critically depended on three men – Thomas Jefferson, James Madison and Alexander Hamilton. While it took an entire nation of enlightened peoples – "We the People" – to achieve such a grand and noble experiment, that initial phase of Constitution-building rested in their mental and administrative lab of political science.

The constitutional Founders got it right when they sought an Enlightenment-influenced separation from Puritan and medieval standards of church domination of the state. The religion clauses of the First Amendment set in motion an America that became even more enthusiastically religious, pluralistic, powerful, and free. As Pulitzer Prize-winning historian Jon Meacham has observed, America emerged in a way like no other country in history – a country in which its citizens could privately and publicly honor its civil-religious traditions without direct government support or overt interference.

However, in myriad ways, the Founders' experiment is being lost. This little coffee table book of beautiful pictures and quotes by the Founders – along with the actual texts of the Declaration of Independence, the Constitution, and the Amendments to the Constitution – is a reminder to the reader that "Eternal Vigilance is the Price of Liberty." Let us be bold. But let us also be knowledgeable and wise.

Gregory W. Hamilton, President
Northwest Religious Liberty Association

The condition upon which God hath given
liberty to man is eternal vigilance.

JOHN PHILPOT CURRAN

DECLARATION OF PRINCIPLES

The God-given right of religious liberty is best exercised when church and state are separate.

Government is God's agency to protect individual rights and to conduct civil affairs; in exercising these responsibilities, officials are entitled to respect and cooperation.

Religious liberty entails freedom of conscience: to worship or not to worship; to profess, practice and promulgate religious beliefs or to change them. In exercising these rights, however, one must respect the equivalent rights of all others.

Attempts to unite church and state are opposed to the interests of each, subversive of human rights and potentially persecuting in character; to oppose union, lawfully and honorably, is not only the citizen's duty but the essence of the Golden Rule – to treat others as one wishes to be treated.

Liberty Magazine

The founders of the nation wisely sought to guard against the employment of secular power on the part of the church, with its inevitable result — intolerance and persecution.

E.G. White

We hold these truths to be self-evident, that all men are created equal, that they are endowed by their Creator with certain unalienable Rights that among these are Life, Liberty and the pursuit of Happiness.

THOMAS JEFFERSON

The people alone have an incontestable, unalienable, and indefeasible right to institute government; and to reform, or totally change the same, when their protection, safety, prosperity, and happiness require it.

John Adams

IN CONGRESS, JULY 4, 1776.

The unanimous Declaration of the thirteen States of America.

THE DECLARATION OF INDEPENDENCE

IN CONGRESS, JULY 4, 1776

THE UNANIMOUS DECLARATION
OF THE THIRTEEN UNITED STATES OF AMERICA

*W*hen in the Course of human events, it becomes necessary for one people to dissolve the political bands which have connected them with another, and to assume among the powers of the earth, the separate and equal station to which the Laws of Nature and of Nature's God entitle them, a decent respect to the opinions of mankind requires that they should declare the causes which impel them to the separation.

We hold these truths to be self-evident, that all men are created equal, that they are endowed by their Creator with certain unalienable Rights, that among these are Life, Liberty and the pursuit of Happiness. – That to secure these rights, Governments are instituted among Men, deriving their just powers from the consent of the governed, – That whenever any Form of Government becomes destructive of these ends, it is the Right of the People to alter or to abolish it, and to institute new Government, laying its foundation on such principles and organizing its powers in such form, as to them shall seem most likely to effect their Safety and Happiness. Prudence, indeed, will dictate that Governments long established should not be changed for light and transient causes; and accordingly all experience hath shewn, that mankind are more disposed to suffer, while evils are sufferable, than to right themselves by abolishing the forms to which they are accustomed. But when a long train of abuses and usurpations, pursuing invariably the same Object evinces a design to reduce them under absolute Despotism, it is their right, it is their duty, to throw off such Government, and to provide new Guards for their future security. – Such has been the patient sufferance of these Colonies; and such is now the necessity which constrains them to alter their former Systems of Government. The history of the present King of Great Britain is a history of repeated injuries and usurpations, all having in direct object the establishment of an absolute Tyranny over these States. To prove this, let Facts be submitted to a candid world.

He has refused his Assent to Laws, the most wholesome and necessary for the public good.

He has forbidden his Governors to pass Laws of immediate and pressing importance, unless suspended in their operation till his Assent should be obtained; and when so suspended, he has utterly neglected to attend to them.

He has refused to pass other Laws for the accommodation of large districts of people, unless those people would relinquish the right of Representation in the Legislature, a right inestimable to them and formidable to tyrants only.

Is life so dear, or peace so sweet, as to be purchased at the price of chains and slavery? Forbid it, Almighty God! I know not what course others may take; but as for me, give me liberty or give me death!

PATRICK HENRY

He has called together legislative bodies at places unusual, uncomfortable, and distant from the depository of their public Records, for the sole purpose of fatiguing them into compliance with his measures.

He has dissolved Representative Houses repeatedly, for opposing with manly firmness his invasions on the rights of the people.

He has refused for a long time, after such dissolutions, to cause others to be elected; whereby the Legislative powers, incapable of Annihilation, have returned to the People at large for their exercise; the State remaining in the mean time exposed to all the dangers of invasion from without, and convulsions within.

He has endeavoured to prevent the population of these States; for that purpose obstructing the Laws for Naturalization of Foreigners; refusing to pass others to encourage their migrations hither, and raising the conditions of new Appropriations of Lands.

He has obstructed the Administration of Justice, by refusing his Assent to Laws for establishing Judiciary powers.

He has made Judges dependent on his Will alone, for the tenure of their offices, and the amount and payment of their salaries.

He has erected a multitude of New Offices, and sent hither swarms of Officers to harrass our people, and eat out their substance.

He has kept among us, in times of peace, Standing Armies without the Consent of our legislatures.

He has affected to render the Military independent of and superior to the Civil power.

He has combined with others to subject us to a jurisdiction foreign to our constitution, and unacknowledged by our laws; giving his Assent to their Acts of pretended Legislation:

For Quartering large bodies of armed troops among us:

For protecting them, by a mock Trial, from punishment for any Murders which they should commit on the Inhabitants of these States:

For cutting off our Trade with all parts of the world:

For imposing Taxes on us without our Consent:

For depriving us in many cases, of the benefits of Trial by Jury:

For transporting us beyond Seas to be tried for pretended offences.

For abolishing the free System of English Laws in a neighbouring Province, establishing therein an Arbitrary government, and enlarging its Boundaries so as to render it at once an example and fit instrument for introducing the same absolute rule into these Colonies:

For taking away our Charters, abolishing our most valuable Laws, and altering fundamentally the Forms of our Governments:

For suspending our own Legislatures, and declaring themselves invested with power to legislate for us in all cases whatsoever.

He has abdicated Government here, by declaring us out of his Protection and waging War against us.

He has plundered our seas, ravaged our Coasts, burnt our towns, and destroyed the lives of our people.

He is at this time transporting large Armies of foreign Mercenaries to compleat the works of death, desolation and tyranny, already begun with circumstances of Cruelty & perfidy scarcely paralleled in the most barbarous ages, and totally unworthy the Head of a civilized nation.

He has constrained our fellow Citizens taken Captive on the high Seas to bear Arms against their Country, to become the executioners of their friends and Brethren, or to fall themselves by their Hands.

He has excited domestic insurrections amongst us, and has endeavoured to bring on the inhabitants of our frontiers, the merciless Indian Savages, whose known rule of warfare, is an undistinguished destruction of all ages, sexes and conditions.

In every stage of these Oppressions We have Petitioned for Redress in the most humble terms: Our repeated Petitions have been answered only by repeated injury. A Prince whose character is thus marked by every act which may define a Tyrant, is unfit to be the ruler of a free people.

Nor have We been wanting in attentions to our Brittish brethren. We have warned them from time to time of attempts by their legislature to extend an unwarrantable jurisdiction over us. We have reminded them of the circumstances of our emigration and settlement here. We have appealed to their native justice and magnanimity, and we have conjured them by the ties of our common kindred to disavow these usurpations, which, would inevitably interrupt our connections and correspondence. They too have been deaf to the voice of justice and of consanguinity. We must, therefore, acquiesce in the necessity, which denounces our Separation, and hold them, as we hold the rest of mankind, Enemies in War, in Peace Friends.

We, therefore, the Representatives of the united States of America, in General Congress, Assembled, appealing to the Supreme Judge of the world for the rectitude of our intentions, do, in the Name, and by Authority of the good People of these Colonies, solemnly publish and declare, That these United Colonies are, and of Right ought to be Free and Independent States; that they are Absolved from all Allegiance to the British Crown, and that all political connection between them and the State of Great Britain, is and ought to be totally dissolved; and that as Free and Independent States, they have full Power to levy War, conclude Peace, contract Alliances, establish Commerce, and to do all other Acts and Things which Independent States may of right do. And for the support of this Declaration, with a firm reliance on the protection of divine Providence, we mutually pledge to each other our Lives, our Fortunes and our sacred Honor.

CONNECTICUT
Roger Sherman
Samuel Huntington
William Williams
Oliver Wolcott

DELAWARE
Caesar Rodney
George Read
Thomas McKean

GEORGIA
Button Gwinnett
Lyman Hall
George Walton

MARYLAND
Samuel Chase
William Paca
Thomas Stone
Charles Carroll of
Carrollton

MASSACHUSETTS
Samuel Adams
John Adams
Robert Treat Paine
Elbridge Gerry
John Hancock

NEW JERSEY
Richard Stockton
John Witherspoon
Francis Hopkinson
John Hart
Abraham Clark

NEW HAMPSHIRE
Josiah Bartlett
William Whipple
Matthew Thornton

NEW YORK
William Floyd
Philip Livingston
Francis Lewis
Lewis Morris

NORTH CAROLINA
William Hooper
Joseph Hewes
John Penn

PENNSYLVANIA
Robert Morris
Benjamin Rush
Benjamin Franklin
John Morton
George Clymer
James Smith
George Taylor
James Wilson
George Ross

RHODE ISLAND
Stephen Hopkins
William Ellery

SOUTH CAROLINA
Edward Rutledge
Thomas Heyward, Jr.
Thomas Lynch, Jr.
Arthur Middleton

VIRGINIA
George Wythe
Richard Henry Lee
Thomas Jefferson
Benjamin Harrison
Thomas Nelson, Jr.
Francis Lightfoot Lee
Carter Braxton

We are now forming a republican government. Real liberty is never found in despotism or the extremes of democracy, but in moderate governments.

ALEXANDER HAMILTON

as recorded by Robert Yates from the Constitutional Convention, June 26th 1787.

The Constitution of the United States

WE THE PEOPLE of the United States, in Order to form a more perfect Union, establish Justice, insure domestic Tranquility, provide for the common defence, promote the general Welfare, and secure the Blessings of Liberty to ourselves and our Posterity, do ordain and establish this Constitution for the United States of America.

Article. I.

Section. 1. All legislative Powers herein granted shall be vested in a Congress of the United States, which shall consist of a Senate and House of Representatives.

Section. 2. The House of Representatives shall be composed of Members chosen every second Year by the People of the several States, and the Electors in each State shall have the Qualifications requisite for Electors of the most numerous Branch of the State Legislature.

No Person shall be a Representative who shall not have attained to the Age of twenty five Years, and been seven Years a Citizen of the United States, and who shall not, when elected, be an Inhabitant of that State in which he shall be chosen.

Representatives and direct Taxes shall be apportioned among the several States which may be included within this Union, according to their respective Numbers, which shall be determined by adding to the whole Number of free Persons, including those bound to Service for a Term of Years, and excluding Indians not taxed, three fifths of all other Persons. The actual Enumeration shall be made within three Years after the first Meeting of the Congress of the United States, and within every subsequent Term of ten Years, in such Manner as they shall by Law direct. The Number of Representatives shall not exceed one for every thirty Thousand, but each State shall have at Least one Representative; and until such enumeration shall be made, the State of New Hampshire shall be entitled to chuse three, Massachusetts eight, Rhode-Island and Providence Plantations one, Connecticut five, New-York six, New Jersey four, Pennsylvania eight, Delaware one, Maryland six, Virginia ten, North Carolina five, South Carolina five, and Georgia three.

When vacancies happen in the Representation from any State, the Executive Authority thereof shall issue Writs of Election to fill such Vacancies.

The House of Representatives shall chuse their Speaker and other Officers; and shall have the sole Power of Impeachment.

Section. 3. The Senate of the United States shall be composed of two Senators from each State, chosen by the Legislature thereof, for six Years; and each Senator shall have one Vote.

Immediately after they shall be assembled in Consequence of the first Election, they shall be divided as equally as may be into three Classes. The Seats of the Senators of the first Class shall be vacated at the Expiration of the second Year, of the

We the People of the United States, in order to form a more perfect union...

Government is frequently and aptly classed under two descriptions — a government of force, and a government of law; the first is the definition of despotism — the last of liberty.

ALEXANDER HAMILTON

second Class at the Expiration of the fourth Year, and of the third Class at the Expiration of the sixth Year, so that one third may be chosen every second Year; and if Vacancies happen by Resignation, or otherwise, during the Recess of the Legislature of any State, the Executive thereof may make temporary Appointments until the next Meeting of the Legislature, which shall then fill such Vacancies.

No Person shall be a Senator who shall not have attained to the Age of thirty Years, and been nine Years a Citizen of the United States, and who shall not, when elected, be an Inhabitant of that State for which he shall be chosen.

The Vice President of the United States shall be President of the Senate, but shall have no Vote, unless they be equally divided.

The Senate shall chuse their other Officers, and also a

President pro tempore, in the Absence of the Vice President, or when he shall exercise the Office of President of the United States.

The Senate shall have the sole Power to try all Impeachments. When sitting for that Purpose, they shall be on Oath or Affirmation. When the President of the United States is tried, the Chief Justice shall preside: And no Person shall be convicted without the Concurrence of two thirds of the Members present.

Judgment in Cases of Impeachment shall not extend further than to removal from Office, and disqualification to hold and enjoy any Office of honor, Trust or Profit under the United States: but the Party convicted shall nevertheless be liable and subject to Indictment, Trial, Judgment and Punishment, according to Law.

Section. 4. The Times, Places and Manner of holding Elections for Senators and Representatives, shall be prescribed in each State by the Legislature thereof; but the Congress may at any time by Law make or alter such Regulations, except as to the Places of chusing Senators.

The Congress shall assemble at least once in every Year, and such Meeting shall be on the first Monday in December, unless they shall by Law appoint a different Day.

Section. 5. Each House shall be the Judge of the Elections, Returns and Qualifications of its own Members, and a Majority of each shall constitute a Quorum to do Business; but a smaller Number may adjourn from day to day, and may be authorized to compel the Attendance of absent Members, in such Manner, and under such Penalties as each House may provide.

Each House may determine the Rules of its Proceedings, punish its Members for disorderly Behaviour, and, with the Concurrence of two thirds, expel a Member.

Each House shall keep a Journal of its Proceedings, and from time to time publish the same, excepting such Parts as may in their Judgment require Secrecy; and the Yeas and Nays of the Members of either House on any question shall, at the Desire of one fifth of those Present, be entered on the Journal.

Neither House, during the Session of Congress, shall,

without the Consent of the other, adjourn for more than three days, nor to any other Place than that in which the two Houses shall be sitting.

Section. 6. The Senators and Representatives shall receive a Compensation for their Services, to be ascertained by Law, and paid out of the Treasury of the United States. They shall in all Cases, except Treason, Felony and Breach of the Peace, be privileged from Arrest during their Attendance at the Session of their respective Houses, and in going to and returning from the same; and for any Speech or Debate in either House, they shall not be questioned in any other Place.

No Senator or Representative shall, during the Time for which he was elected, be appointed to any civil Office under the Authority of the United States, which shall have been created, or the Emoluments whereof shall have been encreased during such time; and no Person holding any Office under the United States, shall be a Member of either House during his Continuance in Office.

Section. 7. All Bills for raising Revenue shall originate in the House of Representatives; but the Senate may propose or concur with Amendments as on other Bills.

Every Bill which shall have passed the House of Representatives and the Senate, shall, before it become a Law, be presented to the President of the United States; If he approve he shall sign it, but if not he shall return it, with his Objections to that House in which it shall have originated, who shall enter the Objections at large on their Journal, and proceed to reconsider it. If after such Reconsideration two thirds of that House shall agree to pass the Bill, it shall be sent, together with the Objections, to the other House, by which it shall likewise be reconsidered, and if approved by two thirds of that House, it shall become a Law. But in all such Cases the Votes of both Houses shall be determined by yeas and Nays, and the Names of the Persons voting for and against the Bill shall be entered on the Journal of each House respectively. If any Bill shall not be returned by the President within ten Days (Sundays excepted) after it shall have been presented to him, the Same shall be a

The Government of the United States of America is not, in any sense, founded on the Christian religion...

GEORGE WASHINGTON
Treaty of Tripoli, 1796

If men were angels, no government would be necessary. If angels were to govern men, neither external nor internal controls on government would be necessary. In framing a government which is to be administered by men over men, the great difficulty lies in this: you must first enable the government to control the governed; and in the next place, oblige it to control itself.

JAMES MADISON

Law, in like Manner as if he had signed it, unless the Congress by their Adjournment prevent its Return, in which Case it shall not be a Law.

Every Order, Resolution, or Vote to which the Concurrence of the Senate and House of Representatives may be necessary (except on a question of Adjournment) shall be presented to the President of the United States; and before the Same shall take Effect, shall be approved by him, or being disapproved by him, shall be repassed by two thirds of the Senate and House of Representatives, according to the Rules and Limitations prescribed in the Case of a Bill.

Section. 8. The Congress shall have Power To lay and collect Taxes, Duties, Imposts and Excises, to pay the Debts and provide for the common Defence and general Welfare of the United States; but all Duties, Imposts and Excises shall be uniform throughout the United States;

To borrow Money on the credit of the United States;

To regulate Commerce with foreign Nations, and among the several States, and with the Indian Tribes;

To establish an uniform Rule of Naturalization, and uniform Laws on the subject of Bankruptcies throughout the United States;

To coin Money, regulate the Value thereof, and of foreign Coin, and fix the Standard of Weights and Measures;

To provide for the Punishment of counterfeiting the Securities and current Coin of the United States;

To establish Post Offices and post Roads;

To promote the Progress of Science and useful Arts, by securing for limited Times to Authors and Inventors the exclusive Right to their respective Writings and Discoveries;

To constitute Tribunals inferior to the supreme Court;

To define and punish Piracies and Felonies committed on the high Seas, and Offences against the Law of Nations;

To declare War, grant Letters of Marque and Reprisal, and make Rules concerning Captures on Land and Water;

To raise and support Armies, but no Appropriation of Money to that Use shall be for a longer Term than two Years;

To provide and maintain a Navy;

To make Rules for the Government and Regulation of the land and naval Forces;

To provide for calling forth the Militia to execute the Laws of the Union, suppress Insurrections and repel Invasions;

To provide for organizing, arming, and disciplining, the Militia, and for governing such Part of them as may be employed in the Service of the United States, reserving to the States respectively, the Appointment of the Officers, and the Authority of training the Militia according to the discipline prescribed by Congress;

To exercise exclusive Legislation in all Cases whatsoever, over such District (not exceeding ten Miles square) as may, by Cession of particular States, and the Acceptance of Congress, become the Seat of the Government of the United States, and to exercise like Authority over all Places purchased by the Consent of the Legislature of the State in which the Same shall be, for the Erection of Forts, Magazines, Arsenals, dock-Yards, and other needful Buildings; – And

To make all Laws which shall be necessary and proper for carrying into Execution the foregoing Powers, and all other Powers vested by this Constitution in the Government of the United States, or in any Department or Officer thereof.

Section. 9. The Migration or Importation of such Persons as any of the States now existing shall think proper to admit, shall not be prohibited by the Congress prior to the Year one thousand eight hundred and eight, but a Tax or duty may be imposed on such Importation, not exceeding ten dollars for each Person.

The Privilege of the Writ of Habeas Corpus shall not be suspended, unless when in Cases of Rebellion or Invasion the public Safety may require it.

No Bill of Attainder or ex post facto Law shall be passed.

No Capitation, or other direct, Tax shall be laid, unless in Proportion to the Census or enumeration herein before directed to be taken.

No Tax or Duty shall be laid on Articles exported from any State.

No Preference shall be given by any Regulation of Commerce or Revenue to the Ports of one State over those of another: nor shall Vessels bound to, or from, one State, be obliged to enter, clear, or pay Duties in another.

No Money shall be drawn from the Treasury, but in Consequence of Appropriations made by Law; and a regular Statement and Account of the Receipts and Expenditures of all public Money shall be published from time to time.

No Title of Nobility shall be granted by the United States: And no Person holding any Office of Profit or Trust under them, shall, without the Consent of the Congress, accept of any present, Emolument, Office, or Title, of any kind whatever, from any King, Prince, or foreign State.

Section. 10. No State shall enter into any Treaty, Alliance, or Confederation; grant Letters of Marque and Reprisal; coin Money; emit Bills of Credit; make any Thing but gold and silver Coin a Tender in Payment of Debts; pass any Bill of Attainder, ex post facto Law, or Law impairing the Obligation of Contracts, or grant any Title of Nobility.

No State shall, without the Consent of the Congress, lay any Imposts or Duties on Imports or Exports, except what may be absolutely necessary for executing it's inspection Laws: and the net Produce of all Duties and Imposts, laid by any State on Imports or Exports, shall be for the Use of the Treasury of the United States; and all such Laws shall be subject to the Revision and Controul of the Congress.

No State shall, without the Consent of Congress, lay any Duty of Tonnage, keep Troops, or Ships of War in time of Peace, enter into any Agreement or Compact with another State, or with a foreign Power, or engage in War, unless actually invaded, or in such imminent Danger as will not admit of delay.

ARTICLE. II.

Section. 1. The executive Power shall be vested in a President of the United States of America. He shall hold his Office during the Term of four Years, and, together with the Vice President, chosen for the same Term, be elected, as follows:

Each State shall appoint, in such Manner as the Legislature thereof may direct, a Number of Electors, equal to the whole Number of Senators and Representatives to which the State may be entitled in the Congress: but no Senator or Representative, or Person holding an Office of Trust or Profit under the United States, shall be appointed an Elector.

The Electors shall meet in their respective States, and vote by Ballot for two Persons, of whom one at least shall not be an Inhabitant of the same State with themselves. And they shall make a List of all the Persons voted for, and of the Number of Votes for each; which List they shall sign and certify, and transmit sealed to the Seat of the Government of the United States, directed to the President of the Senate. The President of the Senate shall, in the Presence of the Senate and House of Representatives, open all the Certificates, and the Votes shall then be counted. The Person having the greatest Number of Votes shall be the President, if such Number be a Majority of the whole Number of Electors appointed; and if there be more than one who have such Majority, and have an equal Number of Votes, then the House of Representatives shall immediately chuse by Ballot one of them for President; and if no Person have a Majority, then from the five highest on the List the said House shall in like Manner chuse the President. But in chusing the President, the Votes shall be taken by States, the Representation from each State having one Vote; A quorum for this Purpose shall consist of a Member or Members from two thirds of the States, and a Majority of all the States shall be necessary to a Choice. In every Case, after the Choice of the President, the Person having the greatest Number of Votes of the Electors shall be the Vice President. But if there should remain two or more who have equal Votes, the Senate shall chuse from them by Ballot the Vice President.

The Congress may determine the Time of chusing the Electors, and the Day on which they shall give their Votes; which Day shall be the same throughout the United States.

No Person except a natural born Citizen, or a Citizen of the United States, at the time of the Adoption of this Constitution, shall be eligible to the Office of President; neither shall any Person be eligible to that Office who shall not have attained to

When you assemble a Number of Men to have the Advantage of their joint Wisdom, you inevitably assemble with those Men all their Prejudices, their Passions, their Errors of Opinion, their local Interests, and their selfish Views. From such an Assembly can a perfect Production be expected? It therefore astonishes me, Sir, to find this System approaching so near to Perfection as it does.

BENJAMIN FRANKLIN

the Age of thirty five Years, and been fourteen Years a Resident within the United States.

In Case of the Removal of the President from Office, or of his Death, Resignation, or Inability to discharge the Powers and Duties of the said Office, the Same shall devolve on the Vice President, and the Congress may by Law provide for the Case of Removal, Death, Resignation or Inability, both of the President and Vice President, declaring what Officer shall then act as President, and such Officer shall act accordingly, until the Disability be removed, or a President shall be elected.

The President shall, at stated Times, receive for his Services, a Compensation, which shall neither be encreased nor diminished during the Period for which he shall have been elected, and he shall not receive within that Period any other Emolument from the United States, or any of them.

Before he enter on the Execution of his Office, he shall take the following Oath or Affirmation: – "I do solemnly swear (or affirm) that I will faithfully execute the Office of President of the United States, and will to the best of my Ability, preserve, protect and defend the Constitution of the United States."

Section. 2. The President shall be Commander in Chief of the Army and Navy of the United States, and of the Militia of the several States, when called into the actual Service of the United States; he may require the Opinion, in writing, of the principal Officer in each of the executive Departments, upon any Subject relating to the Duties of their respective Offices, and he shall have Power to grant Reprieves and Pardons for Offences against the United States, except in Cases of Impeachment.

He shall have Power, by and with the Advice and Consent of the Senate, to make Treaties, provided two thirds of the Senators present concur; and he shall nominate, and by and with the Advice and Consent of the Senate, shall appoint Ambassadors, other public Ministers and Consuls, Judges of the supreme Court, and all other Officers of the United States, whose Appointments are not herein otherwise provided for, and which shall be established by Law: but the Congress may by Law vest the Appointment of such inferior Officers, as they

The framers of the Constitution were so clear that they felt an independent judiciary was critical to the success of the nation.

SANDRA DAY O'CONNOR

think proper, in the President alone, in the Courts of Law, or in the Heads of Departments.

The President shall have Power to fill up all Vacancies that may happen during the Recess of the Senate, by granting Commissions which shall expire at the End of their next Session.

Section. 3. He shall from time to time give to the Congress Information of the State of the Union, and recommend to their Consideration such Measures as he shall judge necessary and expedient; he may, on extraordinary Occasions, convene both Houses, or either of them, and in Case of Disagreement between them, with Respect to the Time of Adjournment, he may adjourn them to such Time as he shall think proper; he shall receive Ambassadors and other public Ministers; he shall take Care that the Laws be faithfully executed, and shall Commission all the Officers of the United States.

Section. 4. The President, Vice President and all civil Officers of the United States, shall be removed from Office on Impeachment for, and Conviction of, Treason, Bribery, or other high Crimes and Misdemeanors.

ARTICLE. III.

Section. 1. The judicial Power of the United States, shall be vested in one supreme Court, and in such inferior Courts as the Congress may from time to time ordain and establish. The Judges, both of the supreme and inferior Courts, shall hold their Offices during good Behaviour, and shall, at stated Times, receive for their Services, a Compensation, which shall not be diminished during their Continuance in Office.

Section. 2. The judicial Power shall extend to all Cases, in Law and Equity, arising under this Constitution, the Laws of the United States, and Treaties made, or which shall be made, under their Authority; – to all Cases affecting Ambassadors, other public Ministers and Consuls; – to all Cases of admiralty and maritime Jurisdiction; – to Controversies to which the United States shall be a Party; – to Controversies between two or more States; – between a State and Citizens of another State, – between Citizens of different States, – between Citizens of the same State claiming Lands under Grants of different States, and between a State, or the Citizens thereof, and foreign States, Citizens or Subjects.

In all Cases affecting Ambassadors, other public Ministers and Consuls, and those in which a State shall be Party, the supreme Court shall have original Jurisdiction. In all the other Cases before mentioned, the supreme Court shall have appellate Jurisdiction, both as to Law and Fact, with such Exceptions, and under such Regulations as the Congress shall make.

The Trial of all Crimes, except in Cases of Impeachment, shall be by Jury; and such Trial shall be held in the State where the said Crimes shall have been committed; but when not committed within any State, the Trial shall be at such Place or Places as the Congress may by Law have directed.

Section. 3. Treason against the United States, shall consist only in levying War against them, or in adhering to their Enemies, giving them Aid and Comfort. No Person shall be convicted of Treason unless on the Testimony of two Witnesses to the same overt Act, or on Confession in open Court.

The Congress shall have Power to declare the Punishment of Treason, but no Attainder of Treason shall work Corruption of Blood, or Forfeiture except during the Life of the Person attainted.

ARTICLE. IV.

Section. 1. Full Faith and Credit shall be given in each State to the public Acts, Records, and judicial Proceedings of every other State. And the Congress may by general Laws prescribe the Manner in which such Acts, Records and Proceedings shall be proved, and the Effect thereof.

Section. 2. The Citizens of each State shall be entitled to all Privileges and Immunities of Citizens in the several States.

A Person charged in any State with Treason, Felony, or other Crime, who shall flee from Justice, and be found in another State, shall on Demand of the executive Authority of the State from which he fled, be delivered up, to be removed to the State having Jurisdiction of the Crime.

No Person held to Service or Labour in one State, under the Laws thereof, escaping into another, shall, in Consequence of any Law or Regulation therein, be discharged from such Service or Labour, but shall be delivered up on Claim of the Party to whom such Service or Labour may be due.

Section. 3. New States may be admitted by the Congress into this Union; but no new State shall be formed or erected within the Jurisdiction of any other State; nor any State be formed by the Junction of two or more States, or Parts of States, without the Consent of the Legislatures of the States concerned as well as of the Congress.

The Congress shall have Power to dispose of and make all needful Rules and Regulations respecting the Territory or other Property belonging to the United States; and nothing in this Constitution shall be so construed as to Prejudice any Claims of the United States, or of any particular State.

Section. 4. The United States shall guarantee to every State in this Union a Republican Form of Government, and shall protect each of them against Invasion; and on Application of the Legislature, or of the Executive (when the Legislature cannot be convened), against domestic Violence.

ARTICLE. V.

The Congress, whenever two thirds of both Houses shall deem it necessary, shall propose Amendments to this Constitution, or, on the Application of the Legislatures of two thirds of the several States, shall call a Convention for proposing Amendments, which, in either Case, shall be valid to all Intents and Purposes, as Part of this Constitution, when ratified by the Legislatures of three fourths of the several States, or by Conventions in three fourths thereof, as the one or the other Mode of Ratification may be proposed by the Congress; Provided that no Amendment which may be made prior to the Year One thousand eight hundred and eight shall in any Manner affect the first and fourth Clauses in the Ninth Section of the first Article; and that no State, without its Consent, shall be deprived of its equal Suffrage in the Senate.

ARTICLE. VI.

All Debts contracted and Engagements entered into, before the Adoption of this Constitution, shall be as valid against the United States under this Constitution, as under the Confederation.

This Constitution, and the Laws of the United States which shall be made in Pursuance thereof; and all Treaties made, or which shall be made, under the Authority of the United States, shall be the supreme Law of the Land; and the Judges in every State shall be bound thereby, any Thing in the Constitution or Laws of any State to the Contrary notwithstanding.

The Senators and Representatives before mentioned, and the Members of the several State Legislatures, and all executive and judicial Officers, both of the United States and of the several States, shall be bound by Oath or Affirmation, to support this Constitution…

…but no religious Test shall ever be required as a Qualification to any Office or public Trust under the United States.

CHARLES PINCKNEY

ARTICLE. VII.

The Ratification of the Conventions of nine States, shall be sufficient for the Establishment of this Constitution between the States so ratifying the Same.

The Word, "the," being interlined between the seventh and eighth Lines of the first Page, The Word "Thirty" being partly written on an Erazure in the fifteenth Line of the first Page, The Words "is tried" being interlined between the thirty second and thirty third Lines of the first Page and the Word "the" being interlined between the forty third and forty fourth Lines of the second Page.

Done in Convention by the Unanimous Consent of the States present the Seventeenth Day of September in the Year of our Lord one thousand seven hundred and Eighty seven and of the Independence of the United States of America the Twelfth In witness whereof We have hereunto subscribed our Names,

The happy Union of these States is a wonder; their Constitution a miracle;
their example the hope of Liberty throughout the world.

JAMES MADISON

DELAWARE
Richard Bassett
Gunning Bedford jun
Jaco: Broom
John Dickinson
Geo: Read

MARYLAND
Danl. Carroll
Dan of St Thos. Jenifer
James McHenry

VIRGINIA
John Blair
James Madison Jr.

NORTH CAROLINA
Wm. Blount
Hu Williamson
Richd. Dobbs Spaight

SOUTH CAROLINA
Pierce Butler
Charles Cotesworth
 Pinckney
Charles Pinckney
J. Rutledge

GEORGIA
Abr Baldwin
William Few

NEW HAMPSHIRE
Nicholas Gilman
John Langdon

MASSACHUSETTS
Nathaniel Gorham
Rufus King

CONNECTICUT
Wm. Saml. Johnson
Roger Sherman

NEW YORK
Alexander Hamilton

NEW JERSEY
David Brearley
Jona: Dayton
Wil: Livingston
Wm. Paterson

PENNSYLVANIA
Geo. Clymer
Thos. FitzSimons
B Franklin
Jared Ingersoll
Thomas Mifflin
Gouv Morris
Robt. Morris
James Wilson

G°. WASHINGTON
 President and deputy
 from Virginia

Attest William Jackson Secretary

Believing with you that religion is a matter which lies solely between man and his God, that he owes account to none other for his faith or his worship, that the legislative powers of government reach actions only, and not opinions, I contemplate with sovereign reverence that act of the whole American people which declared that their legislature should make no law respecting an establishment of religion, or prohibiting the free exercise thereof,' thus building a wall of separation between church and State.

THOMAS JEFFERSON

AMENDMENTS
TO THE CONSTITUTION OF
THE UNITED STATES OF AMERICA

AMENDMENT I[1]

Congress shall make no law respecting an establishment of religion, or prohibiting the free exercise thereof; or abridging the freedom of speech, or of the press; or the right of the people peaceably to assemble, and to petition the Government for a redress of grievances.

AMENDMENT II

A well regulated Militia, being necessary to the security of a free State, the right of the people to keep and bear Arms, shall not be infringed.

AMENDMENT III

No Soldier shall, in time of peace be quartered in any house, without the consent of the Owner, nor in time of war, but in a manner to be prescribed by law.

AMENDMENT IV

The right of the people to be secure in their persons, houses, papers, and effects, against unreasonable searches and seizures, shall not be violated, and no Warrants shall issue, but upon probable cause, supported by Oath or affirmation, and particularly describing the place to be searched, and the persons or things to be seized.

AMENDMENT V

No person shall be held to answer for a capital, or otherwise infamous crime, unless on a presentment or indictment of a Grand Jury, except in cases arising in the land or naval forces, or in the Militia, when in actual service in time of War or public danger; nor shall any person be subject for the same offence to be twice put in jeopardy of life or limb, nor shall be compelled in any criminal case to be a witness against himself, nor be deprived of life, liberty, or property, without due process of law; nor shall private property be taken for public use, without just compensation.

AMENDMENT VI

In all criminal prosecutions, the accused shall enjoy the right to a speedy and public trial, by an impartial jury of the State and district wherein the crime shall have been committed, which district shall have been previously ascertained by law, and to be informed of the nature and cause of the accusation; to be confronted with the witnesses against him; to have compulsory process for obtaining witnesses in his favor, and to have the assistance of counsel for his defence.

AMENDMENT VII

In Suits at common law, where the value in controversy shall exceed twenty dollars, the right of trial by jury shall be preserved, and no fact tried by a jury, shall be otherwise reexamined in any Court of the United States, than according to the rules of the common law.

---

[1] The first ten Amendments (Bill of Rights) were ratified effective December 15, 1791.

Bear in mind this sacred principle, that though the will of the majority is in all cases to prevail, that will, to be rightful, must be reasonable; that the minority possess their equal rights, which equal laws must protect, and to violate would be oppression.

THOMAS JEFFERSON

Amendment VIII

Excessive bail shall not be required, nor excessive fines imposed, nor cruel and unusual punishments inflicted.

Amendment IX

The enumeration in the Constitution, of certain rights, shall not be construed to deny or disparage others retained by the people.

Amendment X

The powers not delegated to the United States by the Constitution, nor prohibited by it to the States, are reserved to the States respectively, or to the people.

Amendment XI[2]

The Judicial power of the United States shall not be construed to extend to any suit in law or equity, commenced or prosecuted against one of the United States by Citizens of another State, or by Citizens or Subjects of any Foreign State.

Amendment XII[3]

The Electors shall meet in their respective states, and vote by ballot for President and Vice President, one of whom, at least, shall not be an inhabitant of the same state with themselves; they shall name in their ballots the person voted for as President, and in distinct ballots the person voted for as Vice-President, and they shall make distinct lists of all persons voted for as President, and of all persons voted for as Vice-President, and of the number of votes for each, which lists they shall sign and certify, and transmit sealed to the seat of the government of the United States, directed to the President of the Senate; – The President of the Senate shall, in the presence of the Senate and House of Representatives, open all the certificates and the votes shall then be counted; – The person having the greatest number of votes for President, shall be the President, if such number be a majority of the whole number of Electors appointed; and if no person have such majority, then from the persons having the highest numbers not exceeding three on the list of those voted for as President, the House of Representatives shall choose immediately, by ballot, the President. But in choosing the President, the votes shall be taken by states, the representation from each state having one vote; a quorum for this purpose shall consist of a member or members from two-thirds of the states, and a majority of all the states shall be necessary to a choice. [And if the House of Representatives shall not choose a President whenever the right of choice shall devolve upon them, before the fourth day of March next following, then the Vice-President shall act as President, as in the case of the death or other constitutional disability of the President. –][4] The person having the greatest number of votes as Vice-President, shall be the Vice-President, if such number be a majority of the whole number of Electors appointed, and if no person have a majority, then from the two highest numbers on the list, the Senate shall choose the Vice-President; a quorum for the purpose shall consist of two-thirds of the whole number of Senators, and a majority of the whole number shall be necessary to a choice. But no person constitutionally ineligible to the office of President shall be eligible to that of Vice-President of the United States.

Amendment XIII[5]

Section 1. Neither slavery nor involuntary servitude, except as a punishment for crime whereof the party shall have been duly convicted, shall exist within the United States, or any place subject to their jurisdiction.

Section 2. Congress shall have power to enforce this article by appropriate legislation.

---

[2] The Eleventh Amendment was ratified February 7, 1795.
[3] The Twelfth Amendment was ratified June 15, 1804.
[4] Superseded by section 3 of the Twentieth Amendment.
[5] The Thirteenth Amendment was ratified December 6, 1865.
[6] The Fourteenth Amendment was ratified July 9, 1868.

Amendment XIV[6]

Section 1. All persons born or naturalized in the United States, and subject to the jurisdiction thereof, are citizens of the United States and of the State wherein they reside. No State shall make or enforce any law which shall abridge the privileges or immunities of citizens of the United States; nor shall any State deprive any person of life, liberty, or property, without due process of law; nor deny to any person within its jurisdiction the equal protection of the laws.

Section 2. Representatives shall be apportioned among the several States according to their respective numbers, counting the whole number of persons in each State, excluding Indians not taxed. But when the right to vote at any election for the choice of electors for President and Vice President of the United States, Representatives in Congress, the Executive and Judicial officers of a State, or the members of the Legislature thereof, is denied to any of the male inhabitants of such State, being twenty-one years of age, and citizens of the United States, or in any way abridged, except for participation in rebellion, or other crime, the basis of representation therein shall be reduced in the proportion which the number of such male citizens shall bear to the whole number of male citizens twenty-one years of age in such State.

Section 3. No person shall be a Senator or Representative in Congress, or elector of President and Vice President, or hold any office, civil or military, under the United States, or under any State, who, having previously taken an oath, as a member of Congress, or as an officer of the United States, or as a member of any State legislature, or as an executive or judicial officer of any State, to support the Constitution of the United States, shall have engaged in insurrection or rebellion against the same, or given aid or comfort to the enemies thereof. But Congress may by a vote of two-thirds of each House, remove such disability.

Section 4. The validity of the public debt of the United States, authorized by law, including debts incurred for payment of pensions and bounties for services

In a free government the security for civil rights must be the same as that for religious rights.

James Madison

in suppressing insurrection or rebellion, shall not be questioned. But neither the United States nor any State shall assume or pay any debt or obligation incurred in aid of insurrection or rebellion against the United States, or any claim for the loss or emancipation of any slave; but all such debts, obligations and claims shall be held illegal and void.

Section 5. The Congress shall have power to enforce, by appropriate legislation, the provisions of this article.

Amendment XV[7]

Section 1. The right of citizens of the United States to vote shall not be denied or abridged by the United States or by any State on account of race, color, or previous condition of servitude.

Section 2. The Congress shall have power to enforce this article by appropriate legislation.

Amendment XVI[8]

The Congress shall have power to lay and collect taxes on incomes, from whatever source derived, without apportionment among the several States, and without regard to any census or enumeration.

Amendment XVII[9]

The Senate of the United States shall be composed of two Senators from each State, elected by the people thereof, for six years; and each Senator shall have one vote. The electors in each State shall have the qualifications requisite for electors of the most numerous branch of the State legislatures.

When vacancies happen in the representation of any State in the Senate, the executive authority of such State shall issue writs of election to fill such vacancies: Provided, That the legislature of any State may empower the executive thereof to make temporary appointments until the people fill the vacancies by election as the legislature may direct.

This amendment shall not be so construed as to affect the election or term of any Senator chosen before it becomes valid as part of the Constitution.

Equal justice under law

Amendment XVIII[10]

Section 1. After one year from the ratification of this article the manufacture, sale, or transportation of intoxicating liquors within, the importation thereof into, or the exportation thereof from the United States and all territory subject to the jurisdiction thereof for beverage purposes is hereby prohibited.

Section 2. The Congress and the several States shall have concurrent power to enforce this article by appropriate legislation.

Section 3. This article shall be inoperative unless it shall have been ratified as an amendment to the Constitution by the legislatures of the several States, as provided in the Constitution, within seven years from the date of the submission hereof to the States by the Congress.

Amendment XIX[11]

The right of citizens of the United States to vote shall not be denied or abridged by the United States or by any State on account of sex.

Congress shall have power to enforce this article by appropriate legislation.

Amendment XX[12]

Section 1. The terms of the President and Vice President shall end at noon on the 20th day of January, and the terms of Senators and Representatives at noon on the 3d day of January, of the years in which such terms would have ended if this article had not been ratified; and the terms of their successors shall then begin.

Section 2. The Congress shall assemble at least once in every year, and such meeting shall begin at noon on the 3d day of January, unless they shall by law appoint a different day.

Section 3. If, at the time fixed for the beginning of the term of the President, the President elect shall have died, the Vice President elect shall become President. If a President shall not have been chosen before the time fixed for the beginning of his term, or if the President elect shall have failed to qualify, then the Vice President elect shall act as President until a President shall have qualified; and the Congress may by law provide for the case wherein neither a President elect nor a Vice President elect shall have qualified, declaring who shall then act as President, or the manner in which one who is to act shall be selected, and such person shall act accordingly until a President or Vice President shall have qualified.

Section 4. The Congress may by law provide for the case of the death of any of the persons from whom the House of Representatives may choose a President whenever the right of choice shall have devolved upon them, and for the case of the death of any of the persons from whom the Senate may choose a Vice President whenever the right of choice shall have devolved upon them.

Section 5. Sections 1 and 2 shall take effect on the 15th day of October following the ratification of this article.

Section 6. This article shall be inoperative unless it shall have been ratified as an amendment to the Constitution by the legislatures of three-fourths of the several States within seven years from the date of its submission.

Amendment XXI[13]

Section 1. The eighteenth article of amendment to the Constitution of the United States is hereby repealed.

Section 2. The transportation or importation into any State, Territory, or possession of the United States for delivery or use therein of intoxicating liquors, in violation of the laws thereof, is hereby prohibited.

Section 3. This article shall be inoperative unless it shall have been ratified as an amendment to the Constitution

---

[7] The Fifteenth Amendment was ratified February 3, 1870.

[8] The Sixteenth Amendment was ratified February 3, 1913.

[9] The Seventeenth Amendment was ratified April 8, 1913.

[10] The Eighteenth Amendment was ratified January 16, 1919. It was repealed by the Twenty-First Amendment December 5, 1933.

[11] The Nineteenth Amendment was ratified August 18, 1920.

[12] The Twentieth Amendment was ratified January 23, 1933.

[13] The Twenty-First Amendment was ratified December 5, 1933.

by conventions in the several States, as provided in the Constitution, within seven years from the date of the submission hereof to the States by the Congress.

Amendment XXII[14]

Section 1. No person shall be elected to the office of the President more than twice, and no person who has held the office of President, or acted as President, for more than two years of a term to which some other person was elected President shall be elected to the office of the President more than once. But this Article shall not apply to any person holding the office of President when this Article was proposed by the Congress, and shall not prevent any person who may be holding the office of President, or acting as President, during the term within which this Article becomes operative from holding the office of President or acting as President during the remainder of such term.

Section 2. This article shall be inoperative unless it shall have been ratified as an amendment to the Constitution by the legislatures of three-fourths of the several States within seven years from the date of its submission to the States by the Congress.

Amendment XXIII[15]

Section 1. The District constituting the seat of Government of the United States shall appoint in such manner as the Congress may direct:

A number of electors of President and Vice President equal to the whole number of Senators and Representatives in Congress to which the District would be entitled if it were a State, but in no event more than the least populous State; they shall be in addition to those appointed by the States, but they shall be considered, for the purposes of the election of President and Vice President, to be electors appointed by a State; and they shall meet in the District and perform such duties as provided by the twelfth article of amendment.

Section 2. The Congress shall have power to enforce this article by appropriate legislation.

Amendment XXIV[16]

Section 1. The right of citizens of the United States to vote in any primary or other election for President or Vice President, for electors for President or Vice President, or for Senator or Representative in Congress, shall not be denied or abridged by the United States or any State by reason of failure to pay any poll tax or other tax.

Section 2. The Congress shall have the power to enforce this article by appropriate legislation.

Amendment XXV[17]

Section 1. In case of the removal of the President from office or of his death or resignation, the Vice President shall become President.

Section 2. Whenever there is a vacancy in the office of the Vice President, the President shall nominate a Vice President who shall take office upon confirmation by a majority vote of both Houses of Congress.

Section 3. Whenever the President transmits to the President pro tempore of the Senate and the Speaker of the House of Representatives his written declaration that he is unable to discharge the powers and duties of his office, and until he transmits to them a written declaration to the contrary, such powers and duties shall be discharged by the Vice President as Acting President.

Section 4. Whenever the Vice President and a majority of either the principal officers of the executive departments or of such other body as Congress may by law provide, transmit to the President pro tempore of the Senate and the Speaker of the House of Representatives their written declaration that the President is unable to discharge the powers and duties of his office, the Vice President shall immediately assume the powers and duties of the office as Acting President.

Thereafter, when the President transmits to the President pro tempore of the Senate and the Speaker of the House of Representatives his written declaration that no inability exists, he shall resume the powers and duties of his office unless the Vice President and a majority of either the principal officers of the executive department or of such other body as Congress may by law provide, transmit within four days to the President pro tempore of the Senate and the Speaker of the House of Representatives their written declaration that the President is unable to discharge the powers and duties of his office. Thereupon Congress shall decide the issue, assembling within forty-eight hours for that purpose if not in session. If the Congress, within twenty-one days after receipt of the latter written declaration, or, if Congress is not in session, within twenty-one days after Congress is required to assemble, determines by two-thirds vote of both Houses that the President is unable to discharge the powers and duties of his office, the Vice President shall continue to discharge the same as Acting President; otherwise, the President shall resume the powers and duties of his office.

AMENDMENT XXVI[18]

Section 1. The right of citizens of the United States, who are eighteen years of age or older, to vote shall not be denied or abridged by the United States or by any State on account of age.

Section 2. The Congress shall have power to enforce this article by appropriate legislation.

AMENDMENT XXVII[19]

No law varying the compensation for the services of the Senators and Representatives shall take effect, until an election of Representatives shall have intervened.

---

[14] The Twenty-Second Amendment was ratified February 27, 1951.
[15] The Twenty-Third Amendment was ratified March 29, 1961.
[16] The Twenty-Fourth Amendment was ratified January 23, 1964.
[17] The Twenty-Fifth Amendment was ratified February 10, 1967.
[18] The Twenty-Sixth Amendment was ratified July 1, 1971.
[19] The Twenty-Seventh Amendment was ratified May 7, 1992.

Those who deny freedom to others deserve it not for themselves; and, under a just God can not long retain it.

ABRAHAM LINCOLN

THE UNIVERSAL DECLARATION
of Human Rights

WHEREAS recognition of the inherent dignity and of the equal and inalienable rights of all members of the human family is the foundation of freedom, justice and peace in the world,

WHEREAS disregard and contempt for human rights have resulted in barbarous acts which have outraged the conscience of mankind, and the advent of a world in which human beings shall enjoy freedom of speech and belief and freedom from fear and want has been proclaimed as the highest aspiration of the common people,

WHEREAS it is essential, if man is not to be compelled to have recourse, as a last resort, to rebellion against tyranny and oppression, that human rights should be protected by the rule of law,

WHEREAS it is essential to promote the development of friendly relations among nations,

WHEREAS the peoples of the United Nations have in the Charter reaffirmed their faith in fundamental human rights, in the dignity and worth of the human person and in the equal rights of men and women and have

determined to promote social progress and better standards of life in larger freedom,

WHEREAS Member States have pledged themselves to achieve, in co-operation with the United Nations, the promotion of universal respect for and observance of human rights and fundamental freedoms,

WHEREAS a common understanding of these rights and freedoms is of the greatest importance for the full realization of this pledge,

NOW, THEREFORE, THE GENERAL ASSEMBLY proclaims this Universal Declaration of Human Rights as a common standard of achievement for all peoples and all nations, to the end that every individual and every organ of society, keeping this Declaration constantly in mind, shall strive by teaching and education to promote respect for these rights and freedoms and by progressive measures, national and international, to secure their universal and effective recognition and observance, both among the peoples of Member States themselves and among the peoples of territories under their jurisdiction.

... natural and fundamental g... to protection by society and the State.

ARTICLE 17 —1. Everyone has the right to own property alone as well as in association with others.

2. No one shall be arbitrarily deprived of his property.

ARTICLE 18 —Everyone has the right to freedom of thought, conscience and religion; this right includes freedom to change his religion or belief, and freedom, either alone or in community with others and in public or private, to manifest his religion or belief in teaching, practice, worship and observance.

ARTICLE 19 —Everyone has the right to freedom of opinion and expression; this right includes freedom to hold opinions without interference and to seek, receive and impart information and ideas through any media and regardless of frontiers.

ARTICLE 20 —1. Everyone has the right to freedom of peaceful assembly and association.

2. No one may be compelled to belong to an association.

ARTICLE 21 —1. Everyone has the right to take part in the government of his country, directly or through freely chosen representatives.

UNITED NATIONS

Ellis Island

Where, after all, do universal human rights begin? In small places, close to home — so close and so small that they cannot be seen on any maps of the world. Yet they are the world of the individual person; the neighborhood he lives in; the school or college he attends; the factory, farm, or office where he works. Such are the places where every man, woman, and child seeks equal justice, equal opportunity, equal dignity without discrimination. Unless these rights have meaning there, they have little meaning anywhere. Without concerted citizen action to uphold them close to home, we shall look in vain for progress in the larger world.

ELEANOR ROOSEVELT

Northwest
Religious Liberty
Association

CHAMPIONING
RELIGIOUS
FREEDOM &
HUMAN RIGHTS
FOR ALL PEOPLE &
INSTITUTIONS OF
GOOD WILL

The Northwest Religious Liberty
Association is a non-partisan
government relations and Title VII
workplace mediation program operating
in the states of Alaska, Idaho, Montana,
Oregon, and Washington. We are
active in the civic, legislative, judicial,
academic, interfaith, evangelical, and
corporate arenas.

Governor Ted Kulongoski's signing ceremony of the Oregon
Workplace Religious Freedom Act, April 1, 2010, with Oregon
legislators and Oregon's faith community.

Religious freedom was to comprehend within the mantle of its protection the Jew and Gentile, the Christian and Mohometan, the Hindoo and infidel of every denomination.

THOMAS JEFFERSON, *Autobiography*

OUR PHILOSOPHY

We believe in freedom of religion but not the freedom to enforce religion, particularly acts of worship, nor the freedom to purge society of religion.

This means upholding both the Establishment and Free Exercise clauses of the First Amendment to a high constitutional standard against powerful forces.

Using this standard, government neutrality means that religion and religious institutions must be allowed to thrive freely, but without its official endorsement.

The First Amendment, in part, states that "Congress shall make no law respecting an establishment of religion, or prohibiting the free exercise thereof…"

Today, some seek to reinterpret the no Establishment provision separating Church and State in ways that would require government to financially support their institutions and enforce their dogmas so as to solve the moral ills of the nation.

Others seek to marginalize the Free Exercise of Religion by failing to recognize that government must have a sufficient compelling interest when lawfully denying or restricting the constitutional right of individuals and institutions of faith to exercise and maintain their religious mission and practices.

Both are harmful to our constitutional health. We believe the Nation's Founders anticipated this tension. That is why they created an internal check and balance within the very wording of the First Amendment in order to prevent the Country from being overrun by either extreme in the great church-state debate (a puritanical vs. godless society).

Remove this balancing safeguard and our nation's constitutional guarantees will be lost, and with it our civil and religious freedoms.

Sandra Day O'Connor summed it up best: "The religious zealot and the theocrat frighten us in part because we understand only too well their basic impulse. No less frightening is the totalitarian atheist who aspires to a society in which the exercise of religion has no place."

GREGORY W. HAMILTON, PRESIDENT
Northwest Religious Liberty Association

Congress shall make no law respecting an establishment of religion, or prohibiting the free exercise thereof…

When a Religion is good, I conceive that it will support itself; and, when it cannot support itself, and God does not take care to support, so that its Professors are oblig'd to call for the help of the Civil Power, it is a sign, I apprehend, of its being a bad one.

BENJAMIN FRANKLIN

An accommodation is not 'reasonable' if it merely lessens rather than eliminates the conflict between religion and work.

EEOC COMPLIANCE MANUAL, PAGES 51-52

HOW WE SERVE YOU

The Northwest Religious Liberty Association (NRLA) works to protect worker's religious accommodation rights under Title VII of the Civil Rights Act.

We believe people should have freedom of conscience to decide what their religious priorities are and therefore should not have to decide between their faith and their livelihood.

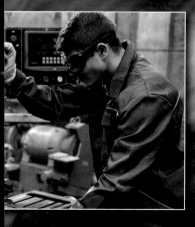

We provide mediation services for those who have sincerely held religious beliefs regarding…

- ⚜ Working on their holy day
- ⚜ Wearing religious garb
- ⚜ Joining a labor union
- ⚜ Promising under oath to bear arms
- ⚜ Eating religiously prohibited foods in prison
- ⚜ Other issues of religious discrimination

We work to find a solution that will accommodate the employee and still not cause an undue hardship for the employer.

LEGISLATIVE
ADVOCACY

*S*ince 1906, the Northwest Religious Liberty Association
(NRLA) has worked with diverse religious and secular groups
who share concerns about religious freedom. We partner with the
North American and International Religious Liberty Associations
to represent the Seventh-day Adventist Church and all people
and institutions of good will to governmental officials.

We work to initiate and pass reasonable religious freedom
legislation, and to defeat legislation that negatively impacts
religious freedom. More specifically, our team of government
relations representatives and attorneys provide guidance and
legislative support for religious freedom bills that uphold the
constitutional separation of church and state and the free exercise
of religion. We testify, craft talking points, lobby and provide
technical support at public hearings and legislative floor debates.

To promote religious liberty, NRLA's staff of scholars, pastors
and attorneys do radio, TV, and print interviews; publish articles,
and speak locally, nationally, and abroad. We conduct public
awareness seminars, symposiums, workshops and lectureships
that focus on pressing issues from a scholarly constitutional
perspective.

We consult diplomatically with countries interested in securing
the foundational ideals set forth in the First Amendment to the
U.S. Constitution and the Universal Declaration of Human
Rights.

We also formally recognize civic, religious and governmental
leaders who champion religious freedom and human rights.

Rotunda Dome of the Oregon Legislature

A MAGAZINE OF RELIGIOUS FREEDOM
LIBERTY

Founded in 1906, Liberty magazine is America's preeminent resource for matters of religious freedom and human rights. Published by the Seventh-day Adventist Church, the Northwest Religious Liberty Association is an official sponsor, consultant, and contributor to the magazine. Through its bimonthly issues, civil and religious leaders receive academic guidance from scholars on important domestic and foreign policy concerns.

www.LibertyMagazine.org

Ways You Can Help Protect Religious Liberty

⚜ **Get to know your neighbors and understand their religious, ethnic, and cultural heritage.** Look for ways to positively engage with newcomers and strangers.

⚜ **Stand against all hate and intolerance.** Determine you will not be a bystander.

⚜ **Join efforts to promote understanding** and invite interfaith and intercultural dialogue.

⚜ **Rely on news from credible sources** who avoid denigrating entire groups and show both sides of an issue.

⚜ **Make a video or share a story on social media** about your personal experience(s).

⚜ **Organize a seminar or symposium in your church or community** and invite a knowledgeable speaker to address and educate people about church-state issues.

⚜ **Read from trust-worthy sources about history, law, and current events.** Anyone can publish a book nowadays. Check an author's education and credentials, and ask the Northwest Religious Liberty Association (NRLA) or other respected historians and scholars for references on individual authors.

⚜ **Contact the Northwest Religious Liberty Association for individualized help** with potential religious discrimination in the workplace.

⚜ **Network with the Northwest Religious Liberty Association on legislative bills** or other religious liberty matters that effect your communities in Alaska, Idaho, Montana, Oregon and Washington.

⚜ **Testify before your legislative representatives or contact them via email, letter, or phone** about the importance of church-state separation and liberty of conscience, using talking points from the Northwest Religious Liberty Association or other well-informed sources.

⚜ **Contribute to organizations that promote these ideals** such as the Northwest Religious Liberty Association and *Liberty* magazine. "Like" them on Facebook and read up on religious liberty news and issues on their websites.

I conjure you, by all that is dear, by all that is honorable, by all that is sacred, not only that ye pray but that ye act.

JOHN HANCOCK

SHORT BIBLIOGRAPHY *(where not cited with quote)*

Page 4   Thomas Jefferson, *Notes on the State of Virginia*

Page 7   Abbrev. quote, Roger Williams, "To the Town of Providence" (1655)

Page 9   PBS Film "The Fight for Religious Liberty"

Page 11   James Madison, *The Writings of James Madison*

Page 14   PBS Film "The Fight for Religious Liberty"

Page 15   John Philpot Curran, Speech

Page 17   E.G. White, *The Great Controversy*

Page 18   Thomas Jefferson, The Declaration of Independence

Page 20   John Adams, *Thoughts on Government*

Page 22   Patrick Henry, Speech before the Virginia Assembly

Page 30   Alexander Hamilton, *The Works of Alexander Hamilton*

Page 32   James Madison, *The Federalist Papers #51*

Page 35   Benjamin Franklin, Speech to the Federal Convention, Sept. 17, 1787

Page 36   Sandra Day O'Connor, "Q & A with Sandra Day O'Connor," *TIME* Magazine, Sept. 28, 2006

Page 39   James Madison, *The Writings of James Madison*

Page 40   Thomas Jefferson, Letter to Danbury Baptist Association, Connecticut, Jan. 1, 1802

Page 43   Thomas Jefferson, First Inaugural Address, Mar. 4, 1801

Page 45   James Madison, *The Federalist Papers #51*

Page 49   Abraham Lincoln, Letter to Henry L. Pierce and others, April 6, 1859

Page 51   Eleanor Roosevelt, "The Great Question," remarks delivered at the United Nations in New York on March 27, 1958.

Page 54   Sandra Day O'Connor, Speech at the University of Northern Ireland, "Religious Freedom: America's Quest for Principles," Northern Ireland Legal Quarterly 48 (1997): 1.

Page 55   Benjamin Franklin, Letter to Richard Price, 1780

Page 63   John Hancock, Remarks on the Boston Massacre, 1774

Equal Protection of Laws

Who does not see that the same authority which can establish Christianity, in exclusion of all other religions, may establish with the same ease any particular sect of Christians in exclusion of all other sects?

JAMES MADISON

Letter to F.L. Schaeffer, Dec. 3, 1821